Yo
Unleashed:
Elevate Your Brand,
Fuel Your Future

Shayna Becker

DEDICATION

For all the square pegs, the misfit toys, the people who have ever felt like they don't belong, this book is dedicated to you.

To my past self, I wish I could wrap my arms around you and tell you everything is going to be ok. You'll get through all your hard days and come out stronger.

Finally, to my family who has seen me through my phases, thank you for loving me unconditionally and making me laugh along the way.

Table of Contents

Introduction

What am I doing wrong?

That question echoed throughout the chambers of my brain like a never-ending stone skipping across a pond. I found myself repeating the pattern of being unhappy, unfulfilled, and feeling like a square peg no matter what I did. At my darkest, I felt like a huge imposter and like there was a secret code everyone seemed to know but me.

What I was suffering from was a personal brand and identity crisis. Finding myself at mid-career and having endured a series of tumultuous company and economic downturns, I felt spit out and burnt out. I didn't know what to do and couldn't afford a career coach that I felt like I connected with, so I did what any resourceful person does. I hit the social media channels and I typed "how to figure out a career trajectory" into an internet search bar. Through that process, I collected and created best practices and hacks to clarify my personal brand and found my way out of the crisis.

The content that follows is the result of that endeavor packaged into an easy to digest process that can be used and reused at any point in a career journey. It's important to point out that this journey will not be linear. I like to akin it to what Mr. Frodo and Samwise embarked upon in the Lord of the Rings trilogy, hopefully with fewer battle scars and giant spiders. At times, I stumbled, faltered, and found myself without direction. Yet, much like Frodo and Sam's adventure, with each setback came new knowledge and with some help and perseverance, all can be overcome.

The intention of this book is to be more than just a manual—it is designed to be a map of sorts with space to journal thoughts and insights while completing exercises. Each chapter is designed to facilitate introspection and growth, providing ample space for you to record your thoughts and breakthroughs. Whether you are a seasoned executive, an aspiring entrepreneur, or a recent graduate navigating the tumultuous waters of career exploration, this guidebook offers something for everyone.

So, dear reader, I invite you to embark on this journey with me—to peel back the layers of convention, embrace the nuances of your identity, and craft a personal brand that resonates authentically with who you are and what you aspire to become. The path may be winding, the terrain unfamiliar, but rest assured, the destination is well worth the effort.

Background

As I stared at the search prompt, I watched the cursor blink. *Blink* – what do I want to be when I grow up? – *Blink* – Why does it seem too hard to participate in capitalism? – *Blink* – What have I been working so hard for? – *Blink*

If that seems dramatic and dire, it's because it was at the time. I was coming off several tumultuous years at an organization that had reorganized every six months, and I was at peak burnout. I had all the physical and emotional symptoms of a mental health disruption: having trouble sleeping, replaying conversations or things I had said in meetings, and wishing at times the earth would swallow me whole. I would lay down in bed and stare at the ceiling because the stress caused me to be numb to anything else happening in my life. Not the mindset to be doing your best work. However, that story is unfortunately all too familiar for many of us looking to find our way on this floating rock in space.

What made major changes in my trajectory and ultimately finding the words and sense of self that I needed was going thru these exercises I had pieced together as my guide. I couldn't quite find the words to describe what it was I was good at or even wanted to do. The person that is writing this guidebook is a completely transformed and more confident person than I had been when staring at that blinking prompt. I barely recognize that old version of me, but I want to wrap my arms around her and tell her that it will be ok. I wish I had such a guidebook when I was starting out early in my career. Having a stronger sense of who I am and who I want to be would have made a lot of those harder years easier to navigate. After gaining control of my personal brand, I did better in interviews and started asking for what I wanted. I was able to land a different job which became a steppingstone to a better career path. I started a doctorate degree and began thinking about entrepreneurship opportunities. Many of those things seemed out of reach for me prior to going through this process.

Not only did it make a difference in my work and career, but it also made a difference in my personal life. I became a happier person and able to show up better for my family and friends. What I have found is that when you know who you are, you operate at a difference frequency. The energy I show up with to any situation has been altered, for the better.

People connect with other people's stories more than products or services. Our attention spans are fleeting, and first impressions matter more than ever. In interviews, meetings, and in networking your personal brand is the calling card that you leave behind in the minds of those that interact with you. It can be a compelling narrative that communicates who you are, what you stand for, and why you matter.

Now, get ready to take the first step towards finding your personal brand! In the next chapter, you'll dig into self-reflection and start to uncover who you are.

A note about mental health before we get started:

Protecting your mental health is top priority throughout this process. Some exercises may prompt deep reflection and bring up personal emotions or experiences that can be challenging to process alone. If at any point you find yourself feeling overwhelmed or distressed, please remember that help and support are available.

It's okay to take breaks, step away from the material, or seek assistance from mental health professionals or crisis centers if needed. It's critical to prioritize self-care throughout your journey of personal and professional growth.

Remember, you are not alone, and there is no shame in seeking help when you need it. Take care of yourself, give yourself grace, and know that you have the strength and resilience to navigate any challenges that arise.

Ready? Let's begin.

Chapter 1: Who are You?

In this chapter, you'll learn the basics of personal branding and the importance of knowing your brand for current and future career management.

So, who do *you* think *you* are? If you had to answer that question right now, would you be able to distill that down into a handful of sentences that really get to the essence of your magic?

What's in a Brand?

There are several components that go into creating and managing a personal brand, and you can certainly add to your list any that resonate more than the ones I will offer in this guidebook. Take this list as a starter set and modify to fit your values.

1. **Authenticity**: In my opinion, without authenticity, none of the rest of this list matters. Authenticity can also be the hardest or scariest to confront because it can get called into question more than the other components of a personal brand. It can be so much easier to put on a mask that is more pleasing to people than being true to yourself. However, that won't get you long term success or happiness. Authenticity requires being able to look at your true self, the inner you, and embrace your unique qualities, values, strengths, flaws, and experiences. You are meant to be here and have something to offer this world. By living in your magic, you create space for credibility and trust while allowing deeper connections with others.

2. **Clarity of Purpose**: Being clear on what you want out of this life is like putting Xs on a map. You must know where you want to end up – even if there are some twists and turns along the way. Getting clear on your purpose and vision creates the foundation for setting up near term and future goals while focusing your efforts. Life will throw many things at you and

your purpose will be the anchor that keeps you steady when the water gets choppy.

3. **Visibility**: If you go through the effort to create a personal brand, you want to show it off! This requires proactive efforts to increase your visibility and exposure to those in your network and future connections. There are many methods such as social media, networking events, publishing content, and casual encounters. Your brand goes everywhere with you, and you never know which interaction will end up being one that makes a difference in your life.

4. **Storytelling:** Being able to tell your story in a straightforward and memorable way can be a powerful tool to promote your personal brand. That's not to say that it requires a degree in theater. It means being able to draw upon your stories and experiences in a way that invites the audience to learn about who you are and leave an impression that will be remembered.

5. **Future Proofing and Growth:** Personal growth is not a one and done activity. This is a lifelong journey as you will hopefully continue to learn and grow to reshape your brand. Stay curious about life and think about what skills or experiences you need to get to the ideal version of you.

By using these foundational concepts, you begin to lay the groundwork for a strong and resilient personal brand that not only reflects who you are but also empowers you to achieve your professional goals and aspirations.

Do the Work: 360 Evaluation

Now let's get to work on figuring out who you are. Allow yourself some space and time to sit with the questions in these exercises. It's important not to rush through these so that you have a strong foundation to build upon. Make a commitment to yourself that you will take care and show up for yourself by creating a safe space.

You: A Retrospective

If you think back on your life, what are the key life experiences that you think shaped who you are today? These can be both positive and negative experiences, because after all it is in the mix of how we got to today.

Create a list or journal key life experiences.

Now, looking at that list, what are the key insights that you gained by those experiences, good and bad, that you find showing up in how you are managing your career and daily life? What personality attributes and values (or fears) did it give you?

Write out your key insights from the experiences you listed above.

Now, let's focus specifically on work experiences and roles. When did you feel at your most realized and valued self? If the answer isn't clear, think about what that might look like. When did you feel your worst? Take some time to think through the different jobs that you have held and jot down some notes about those details. Note: if you are coming into this exercise without a lot of job experience, that's ok. Think about educational experiences or any type of team or role that you've played. If you get stuck, ask someone that you respect or listen to a podcast and read an interview featuring someone you admire and take what resonates. It's important to point out this is the time to evaluate if what you are good at also is what you enjoy. For example, if you are sought out to do presentations, but hate delivering them, think about whether that's something you want to continue.

When did you or what would it look like if you were doing your most self-realized work?

Hopefully after completing the previous exercises, you made some discoveries about your past that can inform your future. We often repeat patterns in life and seek out similar experiences either consciously or subconsciously. It's important to identify these patterns so that we can alter our behavior if needed to make the necessary changes in our careers and life. What patterns can you draw from your answers?

When I went through similar exercises during my intense time of self-reflection, I realized that I was repeating the same pattern of playing small in my career. I would take on roles or projects that were highly visible because I wanted to advance and be seen as a high impact player. What I realized I wasn't doing was bringing that same energy when it was time to make decisions and influence other people. I knew what to do, but I lacked the confidence to speak up and to be aggressive about taking the challenge head on. I would play small and tell my colleagues my ideas or my direct leader after the meeting when the decision had already been made. The imposter syndrome was screaming at me that it wasn't my place to speak up or I would overthink it and the opening in the conversation would pass. I was setting myself up for disappointment by expecting others to ask for my opinion and then feel overlooked when they didn't. Even though I consider myself a self-aware person, it took me writing down the answers to the previous exercises and evaluating it to see the pattern I was creating. Only then, was I able to start doing the work to level up my career and brand.

Now that we've looked at your past, let's turn our thoughts to your future. This is going to take some discipline and an open mind. As I shared in one of my earlier anecdotes, I had been making career decisions based largely in fear. Obviously, there are times in life when we must take what we can get due to economic or job market trends. For purposes of this exercise, I want you to set aside any scarcity fear or what ifs. I want you to go back to the point in childhood when you didn't know the trappings of late-stage capitalism (or imagine a time when) and just dream. Dream big, without hesitation or thinking too much about the logistics of what it would take to make a certain thing happen. Planning will come later, but for now, I want you to sit and think about what your ideal workday and lifestyle would be if there weren't any obstacles.

Some example questions to get you started might be:

- Do you want to have flexibility in the location you do your work and your schedule?
- Do you like to work independently or in a group?
- Do you like repetition of tasks or novelty?
- Do you like to take direction or be the one giving it?
- How do you want to feel in your work?

You can also write down things that you know you DO NOT want if that's easier to start with and then extrapolate idyllic conditions from the reverse. Often if we are in state of burnout, it can be hard to think outside of the negative and this can be a way to break that cycle of thinking.

What would your ideal lifestyle and workday look like?

,

Skills Inventory

Now that you've had time to reflect on your key life experiences, values, and ideal job, let's turn the focus to getting specific. One of the key exercises to understanding your personal brand is taking stock of the skills that you have acquired throughout your time on earth. Think of this exercise like you would taking inventory at a store. What are the shelves stocked with in your personal brand store? By conducting a thorough skills inventory, you will be able to understand what makes you a unique resource. This will also give you the opportunity to address any gaps in areas that may be holding you back from having your ideal job that you outlined above.

A good practice to start is to print off or email to yourself any job description that you end up holding in your career. You can file these away for exercises such as this one in the future. If you don't have a job description and are employed, write one as if you were going to post for your current job. AI editing tools can also help to short cut creating these.

No matter where you are in the work experience journey, you have skills! Skills are acquired at all points in your lifetime. Don't discount some of the earlier jobs that you may have held when first entering the workforce. These can shape work ethic and be proving grounds for later in life.

Examples:

Babysitting = adaptability, crisis management, and conflict resolution

Mowing Lawns = attention to detail, safety, and environmental awareness

Make a list here using the columns below stepping through your work history.

Now that you have created a list of skills you have in your personal brand store, take a moment to look through the table and highlight those that you feel you are strongest in. Put an "x" next to the ones you acquired but have no desire to use.

Next, look back at the ideal job you created for yourself in the previous exercise. Are there skills needed that jump out as obvious gaps? What do you think your peers and prior managers would say are your areas of improvement? If you can interview any and are comfortable doing so, share this exercise with them and ask them to offer you feedback.

Record the answers here:

What are your gaps in skills and areas of improvement?

Craft Your Personal Brand Statement

In this section, we'll take the output of the exercises to craft a personal brand statement that is clear and impactful.

As highlighted in earlier, a personal brand must include:

- Authenticity
- Clarity of purpose
- Visibility
- Storytelling
- Future Proofing and Growth

Your personal brand statement should be more than just a string of words—it should capture the essence of your professional identity. A good guide is 1 – 3 sentences that delivers who you are and what you bring to the table in a way that's easy to remember for both you and your audience.

Remember, your personal brand statement is not set in stone—it is a living, breathing representation of who you are and what you aspire to become. Set aside time to review and refine as your skills, experiences, and goals evolve over time.

Review the output of your 360 Evaluation exercises. Write your personal brand statement using 1 – 3 sentences.

Examples:

I am a creative that takes people's dreams and brings them to life through my skills at brand management, graphic design and social media marketing. I have a proven track record of clearly communicating and delivering results that delight my clients.

I am an innovator that uses strategic thinking and entrepreneurial mindset to bring tomorrow's ideas into today by focused execution and strategic relationships. I think outside the box to bring unique solutions to customer problems that amplify value.

I help nonprofit organizations advocate for change and make a positive impact in communities. With a background in non-profit management and a commitment to equity and justice, I specialize in mobilizing resources, building partnerships, and driving sustainable solutions to address pressing social challenges.

Use these prompts as inspiration but do what feels authentic to you.

I am…

I help…

I build…

Congratulations! You've created a personal brand statement that is unique to you and your experiences.

Read what you wrote out loud as if you were introducing yourself at a networking event to someone that you are meeting for the first time. How does it feel? It should feel like you and comfortable to say. If it feels inauthentic, work on it until it feels like it flows.

Notes

Chapter 2: Communicating Your Brand

In this chapter, we'll take your personal brand statement and learn the importance of effectively communicating to influence and build credibility. We'll also look at ways to elevate your brand using an online presence.

Importance of Authentic Networking

Authentic networking is more than just exchanging business cards or LinkedIn profiles. It's connecting with likeminded people and companies that align with your values and goals and ultimately your personal brand. I have often told my two teenage children that you are who you spend time around as they navigate their friendships. If you surround yourself with good people, good things will often happen to you by proximity.

Early in my career I went to a few open networking events in pursuit of a new job. The one that nearly turned me off networking all together was one where we sat around a table and turned to the person to our right and gave them the stack of our business cards to pass around the table like scalloped potatoes at a family reunion. I was an early career software developer in a sea of insurance salespersons and wealth management advisors. There's nothing wrong with either of those professions or that style of networking. However, it didn't feel right to me because it was out of alignment for my goals and the type of connections I was seeking.

The same can be said for pursuing LinkedIn connections. I cannot count the number of connections that have gone unanswered that slid into my proverbial dm's wanting to sell me on opening my own franchise or another opportunity that was nowhere near what my profile spoke to. Kudos to those folks for trying to hustle and make their dollar, but that's not going to get the type of connections that I want or need. Making authentic connections does not mean only connecting with people that are in your exact line of work. On the contrary, building your network to include a diverse group of industries, perspectives and skillsets is smart business. However, aligning with people that share in your values and vision will enrich your personal and professional growth. By authentically communicating your values, passions, and expertise, you can attract like-minded individuals who resonate with your brand and may become advocates or collaborators in your journey.

Review the ideal job attributes that you wrote down in Chapter 1. When you think about the people that you interact with most, who stands out as those that you admire and feel most aligned with? What qualities do they exhibit that you want to emulate?

> *Write down your network connections that you most admire along with the qualities that you want to emulate.*

Share Your Story, Showcase Your Brand

In this section, you'll learn about the art of storytelling and how it can be used to convey your brand to stand out from the crowd. You'll learn tips and complete exercises to craft compelling narratives to share your story and elevate your brand that will leave a lasting impression.

Maya Angelou has been quoted as saying, "People will forget what you said, people will forget what you did, but people will never forget how you made them feel." I have felt this in my career when I allowed myself to be vulnerable and shared both successes and failures. The most rewarding connections came when I used my own voice to help people whether it be in a mentor/mentee relationship or when advocating for issues that are close to my heart. I had been scared in the past of letting people see the real me and tried to fit into the mold of what I thought was expected. As I shared in the first few pages of this book, doing the work of figuring out who I was emboldened me to put myself in situations that I had previously avoided. The more I told my story, the more people sought me out for advice, opinions, or recognized my efforts at work.

Just like writing a personal brand statement, everything is anchored on authenticity. Beyond that there are several key items to keep in mind.

1. **Speak to Your Audience**: Depending on who you are speaking with, you may need to tailor your message accordingly. Determine mutual interests or challenges that you connect on. Empathy plays a big factor in being able to connect with an audience. Put yourself in the shoes of the audience to determine what might resonate.

2. **Outline Key Themes:** Review the key life experiences that you outlined in Chapter 1. Not only will those have shaped your values and personal brand, but those experiences can also be key in connecting with your audience.

3. **Connect with Emotion:** Emotional connection can be a powerful way to connect with an audience. There's a reason that I included personal anecdotes and experiences throughout this book. They are part of my personal brand and an effort to make the exercises more real. It's also a way to build trust and I'm hoping by sharing my story, you'll be brave enough to share your own.

4. **Impact and Results:** In some cases, it is important not only to share a story, but also the results achieved, or impact delivered to highlight what you can bring to the table. The most successful job interviews I have had were the ones where I was able to connect a personal or professional story to results. Earlier in my career I had often forgotten the connection piece for the audience because it was obvious in my head. I learned that by doing the heavy lifting by explicitly making the connections it went a long way in making the story land.

Craft Your Elevator Pitch and Bio

You've already crafted your personal brand statement and you may be wondering what the difference is between a brand statement, elevator pitch, and bio. While they are similar and are based on your experiences, values, and vision; they differ in their scope, format, and delivery.

- **Scope:** A personal brand statement is the briefest of the three and should cut right to the chase about who you are and what you stand for, while an elevator pitch and bio are lengthier.
- **Format:** As the name suggests, an elevator pitch is meant to be delivered verbally during a hypothetical elevator ride and go into more detail about your experience and background. A bio and brand statement are typically in written format.
- **Audience:** I've mostly used an elevator pitch at networking events or in interviews where there is a face-to-face interaction, or online equivalent and a short amount of time to make a lasting impression. A bio and brand statement will have broader audiences and can be used in any online presences or resumes.

No matter the approach, each has a place and a chance to showcase your personal brand. By having all three in your personal brand store, you can pull each off the shelf when the context calls for it.

Let's look at some examples for a fictional individual named Emily who works in the field of environmental sustainability:

Personal Brand Statement: I am a passionate advocate for environmental sustainability, leveraging my expertise in development and corporate sustainability to drive positive change. With a commitment to innovation and collaboration, I empower organizations to adopt sustainable practices that benefit both the planet and their bottom line.

Elevator Pitch: Hi, I'm Emily. I'm a sustainability strategist with a passion for driving positive change. I help organizations minimize their environmental footprint and maximize their social impact through innovative sustainability initiatives. With my background in sustainable development and corporate sustainability, I'm dedicated to creating a greener, more sustainable future for all.

Bio: Emily Smith is a seasoned sustainability strategist with over a decade of experience in the field. With a background in environmental science and sustainable development, Emily has dedicated her career to driving positive change through sustainable business practices. As a consultant, she has worked with a diverse range of organizations—from multinational to non-profit organizations—to develop and implement sustainable strategies that align with their values and goals. Emily is known for her innovative approach to sustainability, leveraging her expertise in corporate sustainability, stakeholder engagement, and reporting to create measurable impact. In addition to her work as a consultant, Emily is also a passionate advocate for environmental education and awareness, volunteering her time to mentor aspiring sustainability professionals and speaking at conferences and events on topics related to sustainability and corporate responsibility. Emily holds a Bachelor's degree in Environmental Science from [University Name] and a Master's degree in Sustainable Development from [University Name].

Now, it's your turn. Take some time to craft your elevator pitch and bio using your personal brand statement as a jumping off point.

Write your personal brand statement.

Write your elevator pitch.

Write your bio.

Build Your Online Presence

You spent all that time crafting your personal brand and will want to ensure that you are putting your best foot forward and enhancing your brand with an online presence. Using social media, LinkedIn or even your own personal website presents an opportunity to showcase your portfolio of work and skills.

Part of managing your personal brand is managing your online presence. As a hiring manager, one of the first things that I do when looking at candidates is searching their name to see what comes up. Be mindful of what you are putting on the internet, whether it be social media platforms for personal use or your professional contributions on LinkedIn. Even Amazon or Yelp reviews can appear in online searches under your name.

LinkedIn

Most professionals I know have a profile on LinkedIn or other professional networking platforms. The guidance on what makes a good LinkedIn profile has changed over the years, so it's important to understand what the latest best practices are to keep up with the times.

A good place to start is a high-quality picture, headline, and experience summary.

General guidelines

1. **Profile Photo**: include a professional and good quality photo that represents your personal brand. Make sure that what you are wearing, the background, and your expression is presenting you in the best light when being viewed by people who don't know you. It will often be the first impression that many will have of you before reading about your experience.
2. **Headline**: A headline that captures readers' attention and clues them into your brand and experience can drive traffic to your profile. Using keywords that are often searched in your area of

expertise increases the chances that you will appear in search results.

3. **Summary Section**: This section can include some components of your personal brand and values along with your skills and experiences. There's a lot of variation depending on your industry or aspirations. It's an opportunity to show some of your personality as well.

4. **Experience**: Generally, I have seen two versions of experience summaries – either very detailed job history or brief bullets. This is a personal choice depending on your experience level and how much information you want to include. My guidance is to include enough to be picked up in keyword searches, but not inundate any potential readers with minutia of your past or current jobs. Most likely it will be skimmed over.

5. **Skills:** Include skills that you've gained through experiences. There is a cap at the time of publication of this guidebook on how many can be added. Take advantage of adding as many skills as possible to increase your visibility in any proactive outreach searches.

Social Media and Personal Websites

Social Media platforms and personal websites offer another avenue to highlight your personal brand. Neither are necessary in all circumstances and a choice you will need to make depending on your viewpoint of social media usage and desire to have a website. There are security and upkeep considerations associated with hosting a website and it's not for everyone. However, if you choose to use either for a channel to connect with your audience, there are a few best practices to consider.

1. **Platform Relevance:** Know your industry and target audience. Spend time and energy where it's most likely to engage your desired potential connections. Invest wisely because even if free, it costs time to keep relevant information up to date.

2. **Brand Identity:** Ensure your brand is consistent across your channels so that it creates a similar experience and engrains your brand in people's minds.

3. **Show Off:** This is a chance for you to communicate your voice and brand to your audience by sharing what feels relevant. It's an opportunity to create a meaningful exchange between you and your audience. To the degree that it's compliant with whatever employment or academic guidelines, you may also choose to showcase your portfolio of work.
4. **SEO (Search Engine Optimization) Considerations:** You'll want to optimize your profiles and any personal websites so that search engines will include them in results by using keywords, tags, and descriptions.

No matter what you choose to do with your online presence, make sure it's consistent with your brand, on message according to your values, and attracts the type of network that is important and relevant for your goals.

Notes

Chapter 3: Future You

In this chapter, we'll highlight the importance of having a clear vision for the future and how to visualize success.

Visualize Your Future Self

By now you have a better idea of who you are and what you stand for. You've written down your dream job and practiced telling your story. Now, it's time to use visualization techniques and make a plan to align yourself with your goals and aspirations. Let's bring the dream job off the paper and into reality!

You may have heard or read that the brain doesn't know the difference from reality and just thoughts or imagery you're thinking about. There have been many studies done about the importance and power of visualization. If you are not familiar with the neuroscience and research about what happens in our brains when we imagine life as it could be, I highly suggest listening to some podcasts or reading about it more. Manifestation has become somewhat of an overused word. However, no matter if you believe it's a bunch of hippie woo woo, or are open to it, many studies have been done about how spending time and energy on writing down what you want to bring into your life changes your brain. I challenge you to be open to the possibility.

Spend some time now or set aside time later to go through the following exercises. You'll want to do this when you have uninterrupted time to spend on Future You.

The Future You
Take a few moments to go through your answers in Chapter 1 and reflect on your values, passions, and strengths. Review your answers when you felt you were doing your best work and your ideal work environment and job description.

Read the next paragraph and then pause to do the work. Take your time.

Visualize yourself living out your wildest dreams as if they were happening now. What emotions would that version of you feel as you are living your best life? Think through your day as you would like to live it. See yourself happy, fulfilled, and everything coming to you with ease.

Stop here and resume after you've taken some time to daydream.

Write down or draw some of the things that came up during your reflection time.

Creating a Vision Board

I'm a huge fan of vision boards, so much so that I've developed a habit of doing one on New Year's Eve as part of my goal setting for the following year. I've tried, with some varying degrees of success to get the rest of my family onboard with doing one for themselves, but alas it seems it's not everyone's idea of NYE fun.

Vision boards can be done at any point in time, unbound by any rules because they are personal to you and can change with your aspirations. They are a visual representation of the exercise that you just completed and anything else that you want to call into your life. Vision boards can be done by using art supplies and other materials or they can be done online in various tools. I've done both and for me there's something about the tactile process of cutting, gluing, and moving pictures and words around physically that imbues more meaning into it. You can also take a picture of either version and set it to be your screensaver on your pc and/or phone. Play around with some options and see which way resonates more.

A vision board can be done in three basic steps:

1. **Gather inspiration**: collect images, quotes, magazine or newspaper clippings, photographs or other visual elements that inspire and motivate you. They should align to your values and future vision.
2. **Arrange your vision board:** arrange your materials on either a poster board, blank canvas, or online tool. I personally like to use a 12x12 canvas because it can also hold 3d elements and be clear coated to withstand time. Any way that fits your vision is fine. I like to move things around and determine where I like everything as one whole unit, but others may like to do it a section at a time. The choice is up to you, and you'll find your style.
3. **Review it often:** A vision board is not a set it and forget it exercise. Put it in a place where you see it daily. I put mine on the wall behind my desk that I work at every day so that it's front and center and then also as my phone's screensaver. Like anything that you see every day, it can become overlooked as

part of the normal fabric of your surroundings, so schedule some time periodically to just sit and look at it. Take it all in and evaluate whether you still want the same things and check in on whether you are working towards achieving those goals every day.

Set Goals

French writer, Antione de Saint-Exupéry, has been quoted as saying, "A goal without a plan is just a wish." You are worth investing time and energy into beyond the exercises in this book to make your dreams come true. Reflect on your vision board, or if not done, picture what that would look like. What are the steps that you need to complete to turn those into reality?

By aligning your personal brand and aspirations with tangible goals, you can take actionable steps to make them come to life. This may feel daunting, but by breaking goals down into smaller and more manageable steps, it can add up to big impact.

One of the more popular and respected goal setting frameworks is SMART goals. It's a goal framework that focuses on setting goals and objectives that are easy to understand, achievable, and measurable. SMART stands for Specific, Measurable, Achievable, Relevant, and Time-Bound. Many of the companies that I have worked for have used this framework or something similar in their employee performance review process and it works outside of the work environment as well.

Let's look at each of the components closer.

- **Specific** – be clear about what you are striving for as much as possible. It's hard to be accountable to vague terms.

- **Measurable** – define what success looks like for the goal and how you'll measure progress. This will enable you to track your performance along the way.
- **Achievable** – set goals that are realistic given the facts of your circumstances. You can always set stretch goals but don't set the goals so far out of reach that they are not attainable and end up demotivating you.
- **Relevant** - make sure that your goals align with your personal brand and your values as well as your future vision. If they don't serve any of those, then it may distract from your long-term goals.
- **Time-Bound** - setting deadlines for yourself will keep you focused and accountable. It's too easy to drift if you don't set expectations for yourself.

Write down your goals using the SMART framework and set them somewhere they are visible. If you are a whiteboard person, you can write them there and check them off as you achieve them.

Remember to stay flexible and adapt as life or your goals need to change. However, be true to yourself and stay motivated. This is all in service of achieving the best version of you and you're in charge of making that happen!

Write your SMART Goals

Notes

Chapter 4: Now what?

Let's Recap

Triumph! You've made it through the trials and roadblocks to create a solid foundation of your personal brand and future. Now the challenge before you is to figure out what's next.

Let's first look back at the journey we've been on together.

Throughout this guidebook, we've looked at the fundamentals of a personal brand, completed an introspective review of who you are, how to communicate your values, and how to make future plans and actions.

Take a moment to reflect on how far you've come and be proud of the investment that you've made in your future. I'm proud of you! By working these concepts, you can take ownership of your personal brand and your future to position yourself for the type of life that you deserve.

Keep Going!

These tools and techniques will be here when you need them, and you now have a solid foundation to build upon. You and your personal brand are living organisms that will change and adapt. Growth requires reflection and continuous learning and there may be times when you'll need to revisit these exercises to make updates.

Advice I wish I could give my younger self is to take feedback and constructive criticism at face value and know that you don't have to subscribe to everyone's opinion. Ultimately, it's up to you to decide what to do with feedback. Find people that are the type of people that you want to be and ask them questions and advice. Never stop learning or growing, and don't forget to enjoy the process.

I'll offer some final thoughts as you navigate this big, wide world. Others may try to make you question your worth and shake your foundation. I've had many people in my lifetime try to make me feel less than or small. They succeeded far more often prior to my doing this work because I had a less clear sense of self. I still have moments of self-doubt or imposter syndrome. Doing this work will not make you infallible to the complex human emotional ups and downs. However, no one will ever be able to tell you who you are without your permission. In moments when I waiver, I bring out my notebook with my brand statement and values.

And then I remember who the hell **I am**.

Notes

ABOUT THE AUTHOR

Shayna Becker is a doctoral student and working professional with a focus on neurodiversity and organizational resiliency. As a certified Project Management Professional (PMP) and certified Workplace Mental Health Ally, Shayna brings over 20 years of extensive experience in the technology and strategy profession. Her career spans multiple industries and diverse roles, showcasing her adaptability and deep expertise. Passionate about leadership and personal development, she leverages her rich professional background and academic insights to guide individuals in understanding and harnessing their personal brand.